W9-DCV-895

LINE OF DUTY

THE FEDERAL BUREAU OF INVESTIGATION
HUNTING CRIMINALS

by Connie Colwell Miller

Reading Consultant
Barbara J. Fox
Reading Specialist
North Carolina State University

Content Consultant
Kenneth E. deGraffenreid
Professor of Intelligence Studies
Institute of World Politics
Washington, D.C.

Capstone
press

Mankato, Minnesota

Blazers is published by Capstone Press,
151 Good Counsel Drive, P.O. Box 669, Mankato, Minnesota 56002.
www.capstonepress.com

Library of Congress Cataloging-in-Publication Data
Miller, Connie Colwell, 1976–
    The Federal Bureau of Investigation : hunting criminals / by Connie
Colwell Miller.
    p. cm. — (Blazers. Line of duty)
    Summary: "Describes how the FBI investigates crimes to find and arrest
violent criminals" — Provided by publisher.
    Includes bibliographical references and index.
    ISBN–13: 978-1-4296-1273-9 (hardcover)
    ISBN–10: 1-4296-1273-8 (hardcover)
    1. United States. Federal Bureau of Investigation — Juvenile literature. 2.
Criminal investigation — United States — Juvenile literature. I. Title. II. Title:
Federal Bureau of Investigation. II. Series.
HV8144.F43M55 2008
363.250973 — dc22   2007025098

Editorial Credits
Aaron Sautter, editor; Bobbi J. Wyss, designer; Wanda Winch, photo researcher

Photo Credits
AP Photo/Charles Dharapak, 17 (top); David Longstreath, 11; Elise Amendola,
    24–25; The Leavenworth Times/John Richmeier, 22; Mary Ann Chastain,
    29; Monika Graff, cover, 17 (bottom)
Capstone Press, 26
Corbis/Anna Clopet, 12–13; Greg Smith, 6; Ralf-Finn Hestoft, 8; Reuters/
    Andy Clark, 7 (top)
Courtesy of the Federal Bureau of Investigation, 7 (bottom), 15, 19, 23
Getty Images Inc./AFP/Roberto Schmidt, 5; Stephen Chernin, 16
The Image Works/Rob Crandall, 14
Shutterstock/Mike Tolstoy/photobank.kiev.ua, 21

1 2 3 4 5 6 13 12 11 10 09 08

TABLE OF CONTENTS

HUNTING THE MOST WANTED

Criminals, **terrorists**, and spies better be careful. The Federal Bureau of Investigation (FBI) is hot on their trail.

[**terrorist** — someone who uses violence and threats to frighten people]

On September 11, 2001, terrorists attacked and destroyed the World Trade Center in New York City.

In 1995, a truck bomb destroyed a U.S. government building in Oklahoma City.

FBI agents search crime scenes for clues. Some agents dust for **fingerprints**. Others sift through dirt to find clues.

[**fingerprint** — the pattern
made by the tips of your fingers]

FBI agents look for clues wherever crimes take place.

FBI agents ask **witnesses** about crimes. Did anyone see the **suspect**? Can they describe what happened?

[**witness** — someone who knows something about a criminal case]

[**suspect** — a person believed to be responsible for a crime]

The FBI hunts for suspects. When found, the FBI **arrests** suspects and takes them to jail.

[**arrest** — to capture and hold someone for breaking the law]

FACT! The FBI often works with other government agencies in groups called task forces.

Timothy McVeigh was arrested for bombing a federal building in Oklahoma City in 1995.

FBI CRIME FIGHTERS

FBI agents fight the most dangerous crimes in the United States. They protect the country from terrorists, spies, and other dangerous criminals.

FBI agents are trained at the FBI Academy. They learn how to **investigate** crimes. Agents learn how to study fingerprints and other clues found at crime scenes.

[**investigate** — to gather facts in order to discover who committed a crime]

FBI ACADEMY QUANTICO VA.

 There are more than 300 different jobs in the FBI.

FBI agents search for clues at crime scenes. The **evidence** is studied at crime labs. Evidence helps agents find and arrest suspects.

[**evidence** — information or
objects found at a crime scene]

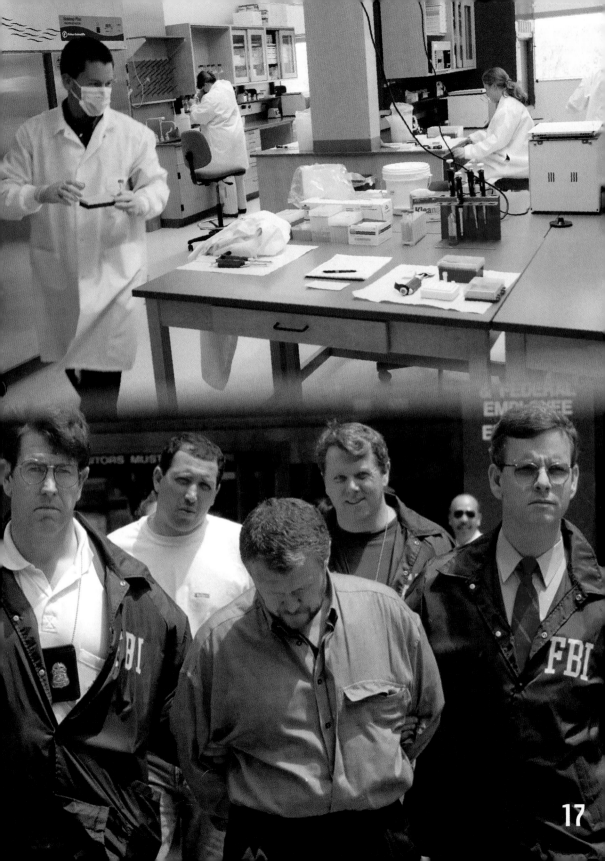

WEAPONS AND EQUIPMENT

FBI agents use guns to protect themselves and other people. Agents train hard to use their guns safely.

FBI agents use night-vision goggles to find people at night. They use **bugs** to listen in on criminals' secret meetings.

[**bug** — a hidden microphone]

FACT! The FBI investigates more than 350 types of crime.

Night-vision goggles make everything appear green.

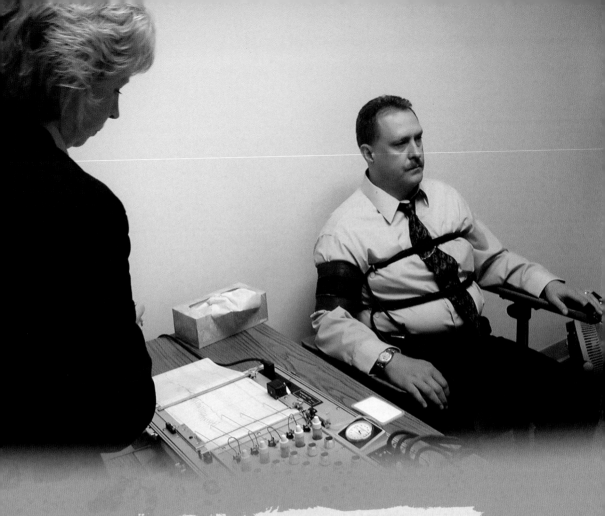

FBI agents use **lie detectors** while questioning suspects. Computers help agents keep track of fingerprints.

[**lie detector** — a machine used to help learn if someone is telling the truth]

FACT! The FBI receives more than 37,000 sets of fingerprints each day.

CATCHING THE ENEMY

FBI agents work hard to find the most dangerous criminals. They usually catch their suspects.

Richard Reid was arrested in 2001 for trying to blow up an airplane.

MURDER OF U.S. NATIONALS OUTSIDE THE UNITED STATES; CONSPIRACY TO MURDER U.S. NATIONALS OUTSIDE THE UNITED STATES; ATTACK ON A FEDERAL FACILITY RESULTING IN DEATH

USAMA BIN LADEN

Aliases: Usama Bin Muhammad Bin Ladin, Shaykh Usama Bin Ladin, The Prince, The Emir, Abu Abdallah, Mujahid Shaykh, Hajj, The Director

DESCRIPTION

Date of Birth Used:	1957	**Hair:**	Brown
Place of Birth:	Saudi Arabia	**Eyes:**	Brown
Height:	6'4" to 6'6"	**Sex:**	Male
Weight:	Approximately 160 pounds	**Complexion:**	Olive
Build:	Thin	**Citizenship:**	Saudi Arabian
Language:	Arabic (probably Pashtu)		
Scars and Marks:	None known		
Remarks:	Bin Laden is left-handed and walks with a cane.		

CAUTION

Usama Bin Laden is wanted in connection with the August 7, 1998, bombings of the United States Embassies in Dar es Salaam, Tanzania, and Nairobi, Kenya. These attacks killed over 200 people. In addition, Bin Laden is a suspect in other terrorist attacks throughout the world.

REWARD

The Rewards For Justice Program, United States Department of State, is offering a reward of up to $25 million for information leading directly to the apprehension or conviction of Usama Bin Laden. An additional $2 million is being offered through a program developed and funded by the Airline Pilots Association and the Air Transport Association.

SHOULD BE CONSIDERED ARMED AND DANGEROUS

The FBI's "Most Wanted" list shows dangerous criminals. People should call the FBI if they see a criminal from the list.

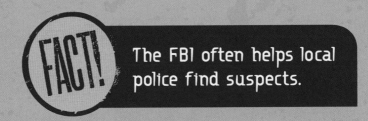

FACT! The FBI often helps local police find suspects.

FBI agents are always ready to protect the United States. People can feel safe knowing the FBI is on the job.

FACT! The FBI searches for about 12,000 suspects each day.

The FBI arrested Eric Rudolph for exploding a bomb in a park at the 1996 Olympics in Atlanta.

GLOSSARY

arrest (uh-REST) — to capture and hold someone for breaking the law

bug (BUHG) — a hidden microphone

criminal (KRIM-uh-nuhl) — someone who commits a crime

evidence (EV-uh-duhnts) — information or objects that provide proof of who committed a crime

fingerprint (FING-gur-print) — the pattern made by the curved ridges on the tips of your fingers

investigate (in-VESS-tuh-gate) — to gather facts in order to discover who committed a crime

lie detector (LYE di-TEK-tur) — a machine used to help find out if someone is telling the truth

suspect (SUHS-pekt) — a person believed to be responsible for a crime

terrorist (TER-ur-ist) — someone who uses violence and threats to frighten people

witness (WIT-niss) — a person who has seen or heard something about a crime

READ MORE

De Capua, Sarah. *The FBI.* Cornerstones of Freedom. New York: Children's Press, 2007.

Hamilton, John. *The FBI.* Defending the Nation. Edina, Minn.: Abdo, 2007.

Ramaprian, Sheela. *The FBI.* Top Secret. New York: Children's Press, 2003.

INTERNET SITES

FactHound offers a safe, fun way to find Internet sites related to this book. All of the sites on FactHound have been researched by our staff.

Here's how:

1. Visit *www.facthound.com*
2. Choose your grade level.
3. Type in this book ID **1429612738** for age-appropriate sites. You may also browse subjects by clicking on letters, or by clicking on pictures and words.
4. Click on the **Fetch It** button.

FactHound will fetch the best sites for you!

INDEX